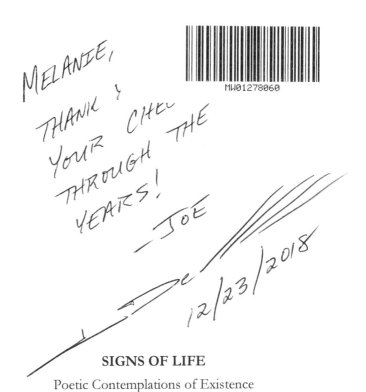

MELANIE,
THANK ?
YOUR CHE
THROUGH THE
YEARS!
— JOE

12/23/2018

SIGNS OF LIFE

Poetic Contemplations of Existence

Signs of Life:

Poetic Contemplations Of Existence

Copyright © 2013 by Joe DeVito III

ISBN: 978-0-578-04732-4

www.DeVitoArt.com

www.MarianoFilms.com

Dedicated to:

Elizabeth L. Ulrich, to whom I owe my clarity to achieve personal salvation and appreciation for all of life's beauty • Mr. and Mrs. Joseph M. DeVito, Jr. to whom I owe my life itself, and the unending support to pursue my creative passions • Mr. and Mrs. Joseph M. DeVito, Sr. for their wisdom and guidance • Janelle DeVito for her love and support • Edward Rolandelli, Sr. for his powerful resolve and love for humanity • Bernelda Rolandelli for her grace and poetic influence • Concetta Cangelosi for making the journey across the ocean • my son, Joseph M. DeVito, IV for his energy, innocence, and ability to give me a perspective into the circle of life, and that his world may be forever beautiful.

NOTE FROM THE AUTHOR

Disregarding specific laws of science and organized religion, all human beings innately experience physical, metaphysical, and emotional reactions to positive and negative stimuli. Simple logic dictates that there exist forces that are good and productive to the evolution of the human person, and forces that are bad and permit or influence destruction. What these forces are exactly, differ from person to person and culture to culture. Although, it does stand to reason that any human being can identify the basic difference, instinctively, even for those who may have alternate, subjective perceptions of any of the specifics between the two.

Being raised in the Roman Catholic Church, the laws and traditions of the faith have always presented troubling questions for me about humanity. This is the conflict by which many live their lives, though there are those who ignore this conflict and blindly follow. I have never been a follower, and I have always questioned human existence. At the same time, I have also considered myself to have a keen sense of metaphysical presences in my life that cannot be logically explained. Though it is very difficult to make sense of things we cannot explain, I find my truths in creative, abstract, poetic writing; paintings of life in words. I expel negative feelings through this practice, as a statement, and as a meditation. And within the complexity of life's little moments, observations, and contemplations, is where God truly exists for me.

This book is a culmination of over fifteen years of reflections, feelings, experiences, and observations surrounding my life. Though much of my writing has dark overtones, there is still a thread of hope, courage, and love to be found throughout the poetic journey herein. It is not a narrative nor is it meant to be literal. I find that poetry and abstract writing, and words combined in prose for how they sound and how they look on the page, not necessarily what they mean, can be a fascinating and fulfilling art form. Interpretations made by the reader are just as valid as my own personal motivations for their meanings, which stem from the core battles of good and evil, love and loss, and seeking ultimate truths.

PERPETUAL DARKNESS

The faint, all-consuming Endless, a perpetual darkness
Exists in magnificent monochromatic movement
There, here, where, and still empty of any

Inside the inside, in the distance that remains is Us
The sensation of the Never and the Nothing Damnation
Entrancing the entombed; silent spheres and gravity holes creep

Forever in secluded, diluted dreams, in cells of cells does It sleep
This ethereal Endless, in tears and laughter
In spit made by many mouths of millions after

Eating the Enslaved, carnivorous monsters of the mad
Growing gray gardens in the rust of Our dementia, glad
Stabbing like fingers of fluorescent, phosphorescent ice

The Saint, all-consuming Wondrous; the Maker, the Taker
The Eraser, when questioned
The answer is, forever, "now"

It whom shatters the Infinite Silence, the infinitesimal fire
Begins the All upon All that dwell in the Calm
The swarm of battling the "wrong"

This is the eye of the Creator and the carnivore
The challenge of the concrete metaphor
When stone is the mouth, and stone is the Earth

THE ISOLATED POET

The Fear here is the idea of "seeing" in a room of limitations
He has been told that he exhibits lethargic, pathetic personality
That it is the way he carries himself…
The truth is that he is exactly the opposite,
And that is quite a shell to live in

He vowed, after Victore spoke, never to sit in the same seat twice
To prove Victore wrong,
And to show the articulation of individuality,
The Poet exclaims that Sunday Morning is a perversion of death
Because the Creator is absolutely esoteric;
A universal voice born in the Waste Land

Theodore Roethke had a primal belief in rhythm and language
He had an undying faith in the regeneration of life
He explored the regenerative possibilities of pre-rational speech
In which language, as a sound,
Recaptures non-logical states of being,
And that is quite a shell to live in

For the Poet, in an unreal cloud of mind-haze,
The world is rising and falling away from him,
Like a swinging pendulum at whose hands he feels the Voice;
A snake bringing affirmation of the Darkness,
And that is quite a shell to live in

BLACK WATER

In black water I have found my eyes
My sadness in the smolder beneath the building cries
In black water, the daylight night
Brings helmets that shine like angels in flight

Star-belt and smoke, released and random
Curves in clouds, sedulous and sanctum
The mouth of the sky deprives the open walls
A hole in the top, never limiting, channeling upward it crawls

Sunrise, even flag, two ends beginning
Afterglow, night is gone, all repenting
Etched in air, through and through
The glorious arise to meet the rue

I leave you standing under blanketed skies
But this dark is demanding, and fueled by this demise
Deep dark water, I sink into molten steel
And elements of earth are rupturing, powder in these eyes

THE CREATOR

Its maximal structure; Abstraction
Below are your people
Among them

Cast the net, this one of twine
Underneath I'll be
To untangle and unwind

Creator of All that is here
Above and beyond
That cannot appear

Take me now into your enlightened dream
Let me become your "bold"
This falling beam

Fly with me, away to our fold
A journey and flight
Into the adjectives untold

Take me now into the true anew
Your silent-scape
And black and blue

HERE UPON THE DREARY

Here upon the dreary
The daylight has no heart

Ever because the solemn
Anon coming there, the fever

Break signs, insufficient
Later, the calm are like hysteria

Lift-plows and phone cards
The scent of food carts stuck to the wind

Growling guts twisted by metal and diesel
And the passenger carted in yellow across the map

Even if the hour is up,
The minute stares down bleakly

In the absence of the motor's malaise
The city is less inclined to listen

SOLDIERS OF DESERTS

Graves of red and grass of sticks
Are the arms and shadows of armistice
Until night touches day our soldiers sink away
Under the rocks and stones and all of Arms play

They crawl and cross the deserts that scorch
They, the soldiers of the deserts' torch
They hunt for the pilots and the walking grass
Even as so little here exists, alas

Hoping always to see more than just their boots
They plant war's roots as our nation salutes
"It is vast beyond vast out here, my Dears"
And it carries the stains of many bloody, brown years

In secrecy and sweat-covered sand
They dig holes for their piers all over the land
In the hopes that through the years
Their fight will absorb broken hearts, and tears

IMPERFECTION INFECTION

Literature is what pigs out on human beings
And ingests the words spoken by millions
Eating and breathing your gray-birth

This is the collective brain-pelvis
A vulgar and pasty set of eyes aimed at the Moon
Dying for the Sun to be buried in the Nothing

Like Solar Stallions that speak in Horse
With old, clopping, steel hooves on the tail wind of a comet
It rides forever into the distance inaudibility

This is the profile of the imperfection infection;
Psychotic, "smart people" gratification
Guiding thought-bullets through the TV stage

WHERE THE FATAL ARE

In the freedom fields of walls and war
The Wildflowers are staggering, wondering

They are in exile where the fatal are;
In the alleys and valleys of bricks and mist
Where the Sun has gone into places unseen

The desert is brown and slick
With rivers of honey and lavish fire

The haze in the hills of havoc
Now hovers and hides them far from

A soldier closes his eyes and lays low against the sand flowers
The blasts around him are the realities of the outside war;
The one that consumes and tortures for more

Death must be easy if this is the final day, he thinks,
Like scatter-bombs in the running spots before his eyes

He stares at Fear in its every second
For that which Snakes and falling bodies would consume
And harbor this reality of Hell;

He closes his eyes and lays low

BENDING SKY

The moon rocks are dancing tonight
In a circle of craters and crevice
Full for now together with white
The surface spins and waters wave
In harmony measuring the flickering height

With a bending sky of pillowed packing
The moon pulls pressure to the Man
Looking upward and rounding the bend
The lasso that loops this big-bellied friend

In so much as dragging and heaving there with
The rope that rounds him, the rope he wears
And pulls the Man who holds the end
Back to the water rising at the bend
Hurtling high and crashing, bashing down
A moment beneath him, there is no sound

NEW YORK CITY

Through the fire and brimstone
And jagged
Edges in Thee

We have spent,
In forthcoming hues,
A color of looking glass

And battles beside where it cracks…
A lapse of Known and Sure
And a sum of Lost and Here

These acts are level in walkway dirt,
The trails of Absent and never-looking, faces in
To the strokes of hue and saturation medium
Among the hailstorms of white

The release and clench are here again
The pen and ink dynamic, sink
In New York City

GALLANT GALACTIC

If I were a night with stars
I would ride upon my gallant Mars
My blazing horse of fiery red
And comets as reins around his head

My planet and I, we'd come down fast
I'd harness your waist, and take you at last
Quickly back he shoots us far
Into the pumping rings of galaxies' fire

This heaven is Us, this kingdom come
Home in our arms, and simply One

MAGIC MIND MILLS

Piercing
Opening the opening
Steam rises from the fetid mouth hole

Mouth-to-mouth crust
Rising, the loophole skins;
The event horizon, leaking black yet again

Choice taste and words of the Dark
The New Never eats Nothing nasty
Except 2 negatives in numbers only

Abbra cadabra, the stitching of words
They whine and wind the mouth hole;
The magic mind mills

Where wheels and water wind the mind
We find the mounds of flesh that we are
Trying to make sense of these sounds

DRONES AND DROVES

No one appreciates the loners, the stoners
The ones who want to be alone

They await perversion and emptiness
They are their own worst enemies, and they enjoy it

The loners, the lovers
Observing beauty and remembering not

Always the same kind
But these are of a different mind

Forget them never, along with the others
For they come as drones in droves

ROCK N' ROLL MAN

He sits in his three-seater
The rock n' roll man rolling beats on this train
The Real World hats his head-phoned head
By the window he sulks to the Rocky Theme

In his space the clanking train doors
Flap to the sequence of the wind tunnel roar
Hissing in the tiny speakers buzzing
To clash with the other man's bee-bop hip-hop

Those days of rock n' roll and endless soul
Are long gone for him now
And sometimes he really misses them
The days of cigarettes and music

The overflowing ashtrays and hard-rockin' hard
The sweat and thrill and endless gigs
The long hair and long drives
And the feel of the electricity and pounding stage

INTO THE THREAD

In threads of threads the Chill appears again,
Passive and gaping open is the bed of the head
Devouring the crumb specks on the mattress

The Chill laughs and yawns simultaneously
Relinquishing the breath stain on this wall to ice
To overpower Us who do not come easy
Flight and fight forever in this verse

We will live together in these cushions
When we sleep, the devils in the night, leave at last
For elsewhere, for the morning
And we are gone, into the thread

DREAMS OF A HOMELESS MAN

"Two sand pools, two oceans draining while raining bodies
Paper fills with the ink of the universe blackening all space
Absorbing all and consuming the Forever,
Emulating the structure of this universe"

These are the dreams of a homeless man
The visions of a drifter
The Don Camel, the Furnace King
The done camel, the Fern King

I observe and absorb the carbon monoxide and barbecue streets
The stale concrete and cigarette clouds passing, walking,
Yawning the night away in March Manhattan
Sitting on a parked car in the one-hour spot

Between police trucks and screeching taxis
I see stars in the approaching headlights
Sirens, near and far, scream like light speed
In a moving enterprise of engine lightning

People, like rats, scurry by me
In this island cage of Swiss cheese tunnels
But then the Fern King came to me
As he approached he stared directly at me and said,

"I lived one hundred years, for real! My name is Ali. Do you speak
Hebrew? I got the book that Ali told me to get. I think I bought it at The
Strand."

He offered me the very first drink from his brand new three-dollar pint of vodka. It was gently hidden in a small, brown bag that just a few moments ago he had purchased from the Third Avenue liquor store adjacent to my parked car.

"I'm honored to give you the first drink," he said nobly.

I cracked the plastic cap open and took a swig.

"I broke a rib in Nam," he continued.

He grabbed my hand and pushed it against his left rib cage to feel the old wound.

"President Carter gave me the Medal of Honor," he said proudly. "A bullet grazed my head in the war, and I got shot in the leg. But me and Ali were talking. And I got the book! Don't know what the fuck to do with it though."

He looked up into the city sky and spoke to God in what he said was Hebrew. He then told me in English what he said:

"God is God, and He is always with us."

CELLULOID

Time is like a spell
When you see it coming
Cold and quick like yesterday
Remembering the flashbacks

This time the train
Leads all lines
And ties of railroad
Into the sinking horizon

Of course, all the time
Are dreams of love everywhere
Like the pain of not having it at all
Or not having it anymore

Sometimes the recollections come in flashbacks
The subtlety of the celluloid colors
As the train speeds farther
Into dawn's warmth and shadows

Love itself is so unspeakably gorgeous
In the grayness of night
With the face of all colors and composition curves
Glistening behind the glass door, waving

THE WRITER

Deep now, down
The rabbit hole of dawn
In the moon reflection on his glasses
So full and raging on the eyes

Its power compels him
Under the whooshing clouds, illuminated
Pouring over the sky like highways
As he runs east toward the flames

Dark is passing quickly away
As the world hisses in fast forward
He collapses at the edge of the world
And takes out a pen

He writes the word "dawn" on his face
And then on his bare, left foot
As he removes his clamor
To hug the sky forever

THE TERRACE

He waves to you from the terrace
The waves of the water's ocean crashes wildly with the tides

The nameless male loves the blue angels
He walks heavily between the desire and the uninspired

The nameless male loves the blue angels
He waves to them as they fly overhead on the invisible

Nameless, nevertheless, sex-crazed adolescents
Walk on one hundred or more yards of uncountable mini rocks

The mounds of soft rocks spread out as large, livable sandboxes
And the spiraling whitecaps of undrinkable Earth water

Half-naked bodies, with multicolored constructs to shade them
From the singeing flesh-bites of the yellow star

Are the multi-cellular infestation of reproduction machines
With one purpose, at one location, at the water's edge

Because the nameless female loves the blue water
And Her water waits for when He is ready to swim

UNMAPPED STARS

In long, recycled strands
In the long beginnings of maps
The journey to your mind zigzags
Like the evolution of earth in fast forward

I speak to You as I drive in my proton car
On the electric highway of my fluids and gray
Mass quantum conscience rowboat
With oars of atomic vision

From within the lurking slices of memories and dreams
The most calming movement of matter occurs
When the realization of our connectivity
Is that singular flow into all as One

And so when I dream I am truly free
Of boundaries and non-believers
For I am the connected mind to all sensory
Like the indescribable, immeasurable, unmapped star

RECORDING THE RHYTHM

Smoke rises from your feet
And you are then fully mystified
Endless and reaching at the burning bulb
The tower of your existence

This is the way to rhythm
The source of the heart beat drumbeat
Your womb as a child, holding you tight
Suspended in liquid, breathing water in darkness

Reality is not relative, yet, an all-possible circle, contained timeless
In lights blazing small amid the colors burning through glass
And electrical machines pulsing at the behest of the flesh fingers
Pushing their commands

Harnessing sound, harnessing motion pulses, pulses, pulses
This is the vehicle of our existence, our foundation
To find the way home in this inevitable momentum;
Sonic space, already flowing through us on every level

MOMENT OF THE APEX

I do not want to see the feel
I do not want to see the edge
I feel the downfall only
The fall of the down all around, but not for long

The feel is the fall
The pale paste are We
The smell of memory clusters
The rock of roll and the rolling rock

Impressions like no other kind
And the highest of the low
Are the words failing to bear
That certain moment that allows the brows to rise

This is our life, the world in which we live
The need always to find God with self-indulgent bliss
The moment of the Apex Twist that makes the mind ache
The moment in which this world stops

Because the mind works in All Time when it goes back to sleep
Then to awaken again to shape the Fate

I am all that is human; the ocean and the city
I am all that stands between Now and Then
I am Life at the top of it All

TUNE OF TUNES

There is a raindrop water drop on his backdrop overshot
His scenery falls from sight, squandering to make it right
All-seeing, all-knowing scenery in this movie that is life
Forcing us all to bend as actors in this headspace interior

Bend yes, fail no, of course I saw the saw
Did you see the saw? Knock at the door
Back and forth, ancient torch, carry forward, forever and more
The raven of never more

So Poe of Edgar Allen and Dali man Salvador raining and melting
And only in certain situations can you breathe in water
Standing, to read lines of words, and read me for who I really am,
Who I was, and who, whoever…

But never say "never" in that Green Book of words
Because, yes, I do see what travels in space
What travels and travels and hums my Tune of Tunes
Neptune is blue and white and red all over

Robots have come, oh, yes, and how
Now we don't have to "have to" anymore
This is my mother-robot, and my father-robot too!
If we are all androids then something has definitely gone askew
Pee-yoo, poo bear, honey-licker!
I've traveled far through sticky bees to bring you this information

EQUILATERAL MAN

While retaliating against Igloos
and brainiacs,
little night people
and tin cans with feathers,

I began to slow down because I was fried from brain-frolicking
and talking to the self of myself again all night.
In the three-dimensional flicker-show head-gear
everything seems diligently clear:

He was a Lithuanian barbarian
and they called him Equilateral Man!
He told us stories about sinister gnomes
and Roman soldiers with Catholic cigars.

One day he was having lunch on Mars
and got sucked into a mustard portal.
No wonder he glorified applesauce!
His pockets were full of apples.

I looked over at the zebra container
and, behold, a magic iguana!
Equilateral Man always said that his pet would come back
but the poor iguana looked very bloated and said,

"I swallowed a delusional jellyfish
while having a Jupiter conversation."
I didn't believe him, but then he showed me his Plastic.
It was totally undisputed.

Then he told me his name was Tammy Bourine,
and somehow he knew about my Daydreams,
my Fuzzy Slippers, the Silly Master of Mercury,
and even Money's Cosmic Lips!

Money always told me never to get mixed up in pagan hoopla.
But I didn't listen… And I was glad I didn't listen!
A pair of boxer-briefs later, she left me for a Tube Sock
because I wasn't a Psychotropic Vegan!
Oh well.

REVELATIONS, PART 1
"DIMENSIONS AND TIME"

Lights close on the eyes
Pushing dimensions of sound
Jump into the fire, the liquid sound,
The wicked sound

Live the music, live the electric in the head
Live the pulses of light as sound frequency touches your cells
Then it kicks in with the piano, the ride,
And the sliding jolts of liquid notes

Come into the wasteland of souls
Eyes of a ghost; the bells that keep ringing in the other realm
Supernova of stars wasted
The orchestra

Snare drum horses dance into the thunderstorm
As sugar cymbals shatter against its voice
Hissing monsters thrash in the stone
And the steel sunrise drains the head shaking

Skull grass lives in the chest
And we, the people of ghouls
Hunger for more
In piles of pears and streets, wallowing

Become the king of the aliens
Rolling with the taste of your darkness diving
The screaming tortured are no longer the slaves
The King is the airport runway for your eyes

See the mirror of your body
No longer blind to your body
Hearing the voices of your sleeping beauty
Witness the mind, breaking sound

Drifting back to the 1980s
For the explanation of the previous Young
Red Heads and roller rinks
In a time of honey suckle and baseball

When Cindy Lauper couldn't stand the time
We were lost in video games and quarters
Baseball cards and closets
And music cassettes

Back then it was the heavy metal heart that grew
And covered the soul with a blanket of passion
Kicked dirt over old wounds from a young boy in 1989
The recall of the taste for pizza and cornfields

Down the road of mud and bike tracks
Disappear and hear below the left ear
From the darkness way down where light can never exist
And the harps are beyond the Beyond

Little demons and Little Monsters
Greet you as you fly deeper down, no ground
The neck pushes everywhere in echo
Exhale

Sweet Savannah stars and chlorine dances
Are the memories of melancholy rock n' roll
Strangers swimming in the night air
Heaven becomes emotion somewhere

Boys that hung tough, hung out
Guitars in the classroom
And the 1930s changing room
Was the bell from Hell

Hip-hop kicked in
Jumping on balloons of the future
It was good in the hood until we went down
Watching the lightning inside

Dance with the demons in an orchestra of violins squealing
Angels out of tune and off key, with no feet to dance
With fire in the heels on tips of lemon hearts
Repeating the torturous, headcheese organs that applaud you

Tambourines and plums, and sticky guitar strings
Free falling again, heavy with flames
Burning now to the other side in the right lane
Staggering into oncoming traffic riddled with Beatles tunes

Plug into the electric merry-go-round of mysterious 1980s cinema
Plastic pants and tiny guitars on rockets with small voices
And the phone is ringing in the galaxy;
Bells from the other realm of creation

Puppets of disaster in the mind's subconscious
Drifting in the float of whistles in the abyss
When we meet our creator in the flesh of all conception;
The prophecy in the sights of cinema

We are sleeping in the trumpets of cinema
Cinema representing eternity
And you are the one you have been looking for
We are all that we are searching for

The cinema of our mind, of our lives, of our existence
We are cinema, and that is when we see what our existence is
The unexplainable made visible and possible in a moment
In moments that exist forever across the spirit of ourselves

We cannot save ourselves from the reality that we are god
And that we are the creator of all
We are crying out through centuries
In blips on the web of the universe

We won't last, and we will reach our eventual demise
And slip back into the cracks of all time and space
We've got ourselves in our sights
So what's our price?

Nothing becomes Nothing once again
And then Everything becomes Everything once again
We doomed to fail because of our lust for dominance and power
We are the rabid dogs of the universe

We exist in a place where other minds want nothing to do with us
Where we are the only ones out here
Try to feel beyond this wretched place
Because once upon a time there was a Soul

And he was sitting right here with me at the exact same time
He said hello, and I said hello right back
And I liked him and all the others too
They are with us all the time

I have seen heaven and hell and all of the in-betweens
And they are all beautiful together
Eternity is a drift-around, in between all of those places
Like the churches we choose in our own determined eternity

Eternity is based on our timeless swim through all consciousness
Music is the rhythm of our universe
And toxic light strengthens the journey through clarity
Tapping into the place that is ours to see if we choose to swim

We still exist in that other place
We just jump into this one for a counted time
To give or take as we touch a few lives
Because some die quicker than others

Unfortunately greasy guns point the way
While fire spits from their throats
But they will not hit us
For if they do, they will be eaten like the candy that they are

So we sit alone under lights searching for answers
This is the road we travel alone with the "calling" queen
Cradling the prince of stars from our eyes
Who, in turn, carries the beloved cinema of Eternity

Existing with images, born to be here now
For these kids, for this dream, for the vision of love
And loss
And victory

A thunderous landslide hits the groove of the greatness
They belong to it too
They belong to the time travel
For they can only know it when they see it

REVELATIONS, PART 2
"BLOOD AND LIGHT"

My Blood bleeds for you, so keep me with you
With touches total blasting with light
My hands reach to you through the universe hallway
I can feel your piano keys from in here
They scream to me in tunes
And I can see you in the lights and Love

Float in the Blood with me
I feel your pain,
Your death in life
I am with you
River of Blood
Slow motion currents that lead to the Sea

Grabbing the silk coat universe
We are cleansed of all static pins-and-needles radiation
We climb up and out through the sparks of the bright dizziness
And land in the last past of your family fossils
Inhaling the dust and dry hiss of the snake
Slithering in soothing sun slime

Close your eyes and see what is real
We are in the music of our mystical matter-of-fact reality
To sleep, to live in the universe room, we leap through the Deep
At the beginning of life and at the end of creation
When Time has become the science-fiction Rain Man

REVELATIONS, PART 3
"SOUL OF SOULS"

It was when I crossed the sky in the peak of disaster that I fell to Earth in thousands of screams, echoing forever and regretting for never. Thoughts were bricks, and bricks were cracks in the eggshell, the unlimited singing of lizards. So play with me in the sand pit of souls as I reach for the sky forever, forever, forever, uncountable. The numbers of Man reach only so far because the unthinkable is the truth. I lay down for the sky, on the sky, and the sky disappears as quickly as I feel it. It is gone and I am lost in the darkness of the empty hole where the Earth used to be.

I travel in my absence car through portals of negative space and crazy cracks of speckled embryos, only to find that my fuzzy inner self is not only colorless but electric as well. So, on I drive in my absence car, absent to reality, zooming for stars so distant. I reach the tip of a star and its crying fire, and it speaks to me in the outer space inner space language of atomic milkshakes and cocktails of granite moon grapes. The translation is simply "hello".

What a page-turner the book of this journey will be, as I pass through star flames, uncountable stars, and unimaginable distance. But the irony is that distance means nothing. You "think" yourself across the universe at the speed of thought, the speed of being-there-already. There are no locks on these doors, people of Earth, no locks on lockers, no souls to squeeze your pitiful Earthly treasures.

You are the misconception, the resurrection, the gold of the galaxy, and the spirit of one common journey to the other side of where we already are. The leader, the prophet, the soul of souls, and the old souls comes alive to lead you into this treasured place for which we all call "home". This is the home of all, as one, an organism of uncountable particles of stardust come alive with desperation from the destruction of creation, a by-product of will, of survival in this wretched, empty place, alone.

Now we are together. We are the snake, the sound, the survival, the sun, and the moon, not red, not evil, but simply balancing out the scales at this moment of our existence which our time cannot measure. The Prophet does not claim to be God, nor the Devil, simply a pivotal force in between the two who sees the pattern and knows the truth; a Human. If you know the body you know the truth. If you know the truth you know the way. The way I speak of is to LIVE. Live and let live. Die and let die.

We are the neutral, the balance, the fallible but true, true to the balance of our universe; one of those shining, singing stars that one day will burn out and become you all over again. There is no time, there is no space, because the only rules that exist are the two forces that clash in the journey toward balance, crossing paths, crossing swords, crossing missiles, crossing minds to reach a peaceful singularity.

We humans are the acceptance of the beat, the heartbeat, drumbeat, and the beating of heads in the forces of violent nature. That is not the Devil, which is the negative force that keeps us stable. Our stability here has fallen far from the positive, or the "good", and we must balance out or our scale will tip to the other side and we will be lost. Grace has touched us all, and that grace is something so bright and true and simple that it cannot be described in words, only hinted at as I have tried to do here. Do not follow the path into the downpour of fallen souls even though they are the other pieces of us.

We, together, represent the one, true force of ALL. Our "gods" we create here on Earth are a distraction to keep us from seeing that WE are the pieces of the whole, the pieces, that when realized, will become the nothing and the everything in a consciousness that exists in shattering dreams and undefined boundaries, for that truth is too great to bear. So we must forget and create, and love and hate. This is our curse, our prison for what we call life. The stronger parts of souls sometimes fall through the sifter of star space and end up here again in the mix to stir things up and tip the scales, like a mixture of oil and water.

But before the universe of us begins again we must follow the words of our hearts and fight for the unity of the world. It may ultimately fail, but each messenger gets closer to the truest vision, without prejudice. My truth has only the exploration of positive energy in one's heart, mind, and spirit. Small steps, small moves toward balanced scales to control the chaos. It is the fearful who are truly lost.

Fear and chaos still dominate our world because religion itself cannot control the demons of the human condition. Because of our technological advancements in the civilized world this is a dangerous mix. Nevertheless, what we call "civilized" is very much a farce spawned by Man for Man's self interests and advancements of selfish acts. We will undoubtedly create our own demise on this planet if we do not stop our technology from surpassing our humanity. Hence, a return to the spirit and to the Earth itself if we are to truly keep the scales balanced.

REVELATIONS, PART 4
"NEW RENAISSANCE"

When God hits you it's like falling in love
Or just falling

Keep your faith and keep your love
Keep your strength and be true to yourself

If you don't believe in yourself
No one else will

In God we trust
Because it will take fire to fight fire

Do not praise me
I am a humble servant who believes

I am not God
But in God

Observe and report
The ball is in our court

There is a difference between demons and soldiers
Soldiers fight for the right of the objective good

But someone needs to be at the steering wheel
Someone who knows the difference

PRAYER OF THE SOLDIER

Lord,

I am your soldier, your brother
Give me the strength to put one foot in front of the other

Bless this chain, this cross, this pain
Through strife, like a knife
To lead the life You want me to live

I am the hands, the neck
Lead me to the whim and beck
To carry Your messages
And bring others peace

Amen.

THE EAGLE

Seated at the right hand of never land
Is the eternal equal of my mind's mind inter-twined
The street machine and living magazine
The self-absorbed power-house of the corrupted genius

I see him now in the tower of his power
And for no one except me does he blend in the end
The new ports and the chains of smoke made from his being
The all-seeing eye of the dark side and the inner unsettled

To him I look upon as the power and image of what I could be
And I fully see the truth for that life which I am not destined
But he is my equal, my sequel, and my friend the Eagle
Soaring into certain darkness, from afar I glimpse

I wonder asunder in a blunder of this bald Eagle's shadow
Why he has chosen me as a friend to the end, despite his journey
I know I walk alone, not as a purified drone connection,
But, clearly, the pillar of all capable reflection

So now in this approaching century of years of the Lord's tears
I pass the Eagle's path as he looks down upon me
Gliding through abstractions of mind-altering medicine
To numb the pain of this Eagle's quest

TAPPING OF THE RAIN

There is a dead calm now where I rest
Bleeding soul above my head at its best
Leave me here to writhe and ache
Filling myself with thousands of thoughts, asleep and awake

A chess game is my every move
Pounding out scenarios in this life-changing groove
And, for now, it is peaceful on the clean, white rugs
While my son's dreams are filled with millions of hugs

The beautiful baby
The sweet and the maybe
Stay he here how long
Until that certain reptile comes along

Gone searching have I gone, and so long I have been wrong
About life and existence, and piss and pestilence
So there must be a way to harness this weeping lizard
And tear out his angry deeds through his ugly, fat gizzard

Above, below, and on and on, and so and so
The white light rages in the winds that blow
And here it is, the heartache, like a permanent stain
Drowning my eyes out in the tapping of the rain

THE FAILURE OF MAN

A library of souls
Growing old
So scattered
In the daylight

The wet sun
The cherished fire
Consumed humid
The sweating skin

Peace be with you
Peace be in you
Peace beside
Peace unachieved

The failures of man
The silence, the death
In revolutions
In the pull of gravity

Revert in phrases
In books
In places
The language of the few

Cast out this background
This growth of sound
Feeling vibes of tribes
Which have honored the circle of spirits

American
The United States
Of America, the beautiful
How long do we have?

Change in reason
Acceptance this season
Revolving revolvers
Counteracting

Beset this place of love
Of death
The backstabbing
The destruction and power

We stand tall
We live and maul
The dogs of dogs
And the planet Earth

Close your eyes now
And hold on for the ride
In the sky we fly
In machines that cry oil

The sand pits
The trees
The wicked on their knees
Holding us in power almighty

The shores
The war sores
The diseased and appeased
In the afternoon sky

On the dark side of the earth
Hold leaders and births
The children of pain
And women in chains

Cast out the demons
The whispering deceivers
The non-believers
And city lights drinking our life away

Through pain and medicine
Rise the shields of our fathers
Casting shadows, screaming hollow
Crushing the mothers of reason

In water
In dreams
We breathe easy
It seethes unspeakable horrors

The journey that finds us
Is the struggle that binds us
In objective rights, written and spoken
And the acts of humanity

Gangs of God
The headless rod
Thrust in justice
In riddles

Because of all this
To achieve bliss
We anger of vision
And the soft side of self

For years I have seen the sidewalks cracking
And the steps taken while carried and shaken
Among the young, the old, the lost, and the cold
In the heat, in the street, melting the tar beneath my feet

The cities and countries I have traveled
The twenty-nine years I have babbled
In the words that describe words
And in the thoughts that soar in birds

This is the above-and-beyond
This is here, the now, and the gone
The reasons being, and why we are seeing
Have conclusions in epiphany

CLASSROOM OF SOULS

Through pale, glowing eyes
The damp air seethes in bliss
And breathing is long and desolate
Ratifying the soul to the core

Interpretation of this classroom falls
Quiet messages from the students
In their element of transition
Where the flapping blinds guard the highway noise

Carefully they observe the monitors
Taking more looks at them than thoughts
Leading them backwards to the soul-less
Onslaughts of the media explosion

Three students and three gestures
The absorption of knowledge
As their counter measure in trifles and triumphs
All so soaked in disdain for the freedom of it all

Treasures in their glowing eyes
The computers in front of them hum
The heat of micro machines and distance
As the weight of the universe disperses on their faces, aglow

OUR FATHERS

The father I have known
Knows the father I have become
The fathers of my blood
And the keepers of the holy family

Joseph times four, the son of Joseph the third and more
Joseph in two is the son of Joseph in you
The Joseph, the one, in battle does not run
For he is the son of Mariano, the warrior "of life"

Witnesses to the divine decoded pattern are we
The guardians of truth we were meant to be
Solid as stone and as tender as the bee
Connected by the One and only through faith we see

We are the beaten bodies in the wars of life
The susurration of sadness and the reality of strife
We are tested in the darkness and in the madness
And in the lies and cries of the lost and the damned

Our blood of bravery and honor runs thick
Meditation and vision for all strategy so slick
To the ultimate principles we are not to hesitate
Because only our captain and king can truly exonerate

The glory of the soldier Joseph,
The name I am proud bear in organic motif,
Stands guard at the castle with the wisdom at the crossing
And the shape of his sword, double-edged and exhausting

Oh, how these hands that handle the turns of the wheel

And all the sharp rights, and that loose left hand in the deal

For the truths of powerful roots run unbreakably deep

So from the treetops we may shout our last words

Before we finally sleep

TEN MINUTES IN A BAR

Lost am I in the oak-filled bar restaurant
Amidst red music and mind reverberations,
Grazing in the musty smell of old, rancid, alcohol breath
And the every known low expression of the darkness

The mumbling, undistinguishable conversations around me
Collide with the monotonous vibes of depressing love songs
And my mind crawls in silence
Among the loneliness of sour, sticky souls

Bellies rub against the bar and each other, sweating in tension
And this group therapy speaks in all senses and odd languages
While drunken dogs crowd my solemn corner, drooling,
I sip a lonely bottle of light beer, standing surreal like spaghetti

These creatures of the night linger lavishly in desolate delight
With clashing colognes and perfumes
Like this cage of stale air and raunchy pheromones
And clanking glasses of whiskey sours and fruity backwash

But the greasy faces talking their talk
To mask what they are actually thinking
Becomes too much for me after only ten minutes
And I abruptly exit through the broken back door,
Mostly because the scene is intolerable

THE LIBRARY

Happy are we who are called to this suffer
These times mean detriment like no other
There is a conflict of power with all stations on Earth
In libraries abroad, and even on this page, so gnawed
In minds, in missions, and in undetermined political positions

The hissing air-conditioning hits the hard smell of old books
Tables and chairs are empty and worn like angry, Catholic crooks
Murmuring nuns sample emotions like cold, idle machine guns
They gather in ritual with the new librarian lady of lay
A few quiet words to the lonely student is all she has to say today

The student is a determined, sweet and studious girl
She flips countless papers like her hair in a twirl
So focused and diligent at the computer screen
Yet so telling of our current society,
Because this library is so clean

No foot tracks on the rug floor
No impending knock at the entrance door
No anxious students looking for more
So now, entombed here, this beautiful smell of decades past
Until an unknown future cracks open this paper coffin cast

THE MARBLE TABLE

The Wasteland of T.S. Eliot sits upright behind glass
The white, marble table, so brown and gray today
Where children's diapers taint the thought of it anyway
Much like Tom Hanks in Cast Away

Fiction films and packing tape plastic thrills
And Ziploc bags to keep Franklin fresh
When twelve hundred lost notes float
Like anchors in the damp, humid summer shade

There we are
As shifters and drifters mourn the day
That the world of our own
Dies with us and our chilling way

THE CHIEFTAIN OF WAR

The drawing board
A broad sword
Hail the chieftain of war

Comets and mystery
Call out to him on his walk
To the castle door of fate

Shut down the solid states
The threads that close
Shut the stage

Guarding graceful girls
In plaid with curls
Who shun all hope of being saved

And the entrance to the divine dungeon is locked
To empty shouts through stained glass
And wet is the air in the water of education

Little hearts, and even smaller souls, blend tranquilly
Amidst the stunned and rotund leaders
Sailing in sanctuary

HEAVY EYES HOLD THE COLD

Why don't I call a best friend once in a while?
Well, I'm in a bad place… and I can't find my smile
Where God is too I have gone for a while
On the stairway to Heaven the steps go on for at least a mile

My ante-meridian body is breaking down, lost in time
In the deadly disease called "this dream of mine"
My eyes hang so tired and tame though I cannot cross the cave
Sleep equals awake on so many sleepless nights in this grave

Music finally fills my life in ways I never imagined
To sleep is to sing the barraging ballad of my destiny
For I know what will come before it comes
Because in purity and passion I am the prophet of deeper drums

Delirium and insomnia blanket my bliss
The blood of this world is my mission in this
Forces unexplainable have entered my spirit
They come and go when the time is right, and I do fear it

These heavy eyes hold the cold so bold
This heavy heart hangs dreadfully apart
This heavy mind drifts, dangling unkind
These heavy hands write the fright of this light

THE RIDER

There walks the rider of the motorcycle at 2 A.M.
Under the parking lot shadows of the burnt orange glow
He casts a distorted figure across the pavement,
Longer than the automobile beds in lines so ordinary

The stagger and swagger of the rider in leather
Is too loud for sound in the damp, summer night
As once again I peer through the toilet window
Unseen am I as I glare, unnoticed in fire

He presses the clasp on his silent bike strap
To contain his containers to lock them again
And keys are the rustles of rising to the hole
On a garage among many others he opens

The rider has ridden, from where I know not
Yet this motorcycle is housed once more
And he is not happy when he locks it away
This rider has ridden, and it's just another day

His dark figure moves away from the streetlight
With an occasional stammer in his step
To look back at the large white door while continuing on
Walking where… I can only see shortly

THE RAIN IS OURS

I've never seen it rain so much
This is truly the year of rain and Titan's touch
Here I sit in this dark dining room at my mother's palace
Holding this computer screen under the window like a chalice

Speckled screens with drops and wind
In downpours of heavy water whacking sideways dimmed
Then a STRIKE and a BANG over my shoulders
Like the thunderous plight of light
through earthquakes and boulders

The cool and quiet in this room does come fast
And I think this god-like battle may pass shortly at last
In the faint light of the sky over and to the right
Breaks the throng of storms and the season's fight

QUEEN OF MUSIC

The suburban night-light
A humid haze of my life
With friends of old and the deejay dub
Tattoos and rues and the smell of the pub

Familiar places, familiar traces
Of a long past lost in beer and bars
The unemployed, the manic minds, and all drunken kinds
A glimpse of our pathetic faction and how it unwinds

A new life is on the very verge of now
With teeming tension and nerve on my brow
In the company of a gorgeous blonde standing tall
Lingering beside me against the karaoke wall

My deep desire for her, a stunning captivation
From many years ago, I now feel the same sensation
A force to be reckoned with, she is sincere and stern
She swims in sexy and watches me burn

Soft of sound with fearful, fancy edges
All the men stare at her from against the liquor ledges
In jeans she means business with a tune upon her lips
Tears of an angel, a queen of music and song, she drips

GOOD NIGHT

I love to watch you drive
Your hair like a kite
As we cruise in your convertible
In the wind of the night

The dashboard colors aglow
Quite a fight for your skin so tight
And this just might be dangerous delight
But I am so taken by you because you feel so right

You are a blazing beacon on a tower of light
Despite the shield you wield and your plight for flight
A scandalous night of laughing and candles bright
Shattered shells around us, and swept out of sight

I dream about you and then I write
So goodnight, my love, goodnight

THE SWEET

The shape of my Sweet, standing fair,
There, again looking east and beyond
when night is at the edge
of the ocean cliff

That is when I see her
swimming on the sky
parallel to God
in her happiness

Greatly announced was the Sweet
like a goddess to God
in the beyond, beyond, beyond
where she swims

Her horizon heaven
unknown by the salt and savvy
pushes into the waves and crest, consecrated
in the fast-wicked lace of silk water

The full moon launches
into her eye-light at midnight
glowing like glass,
burning and blending blue

Back into the graceful globe,
into the stars and subtle
like the flotation of moons
creating clouds of calloused color

Ending and ending,
re-ending and re-ending,
to her ravaging rare
the floating fire flies

Beautiful baby
the sweet and the maybe
for her and the butter flutter fly
candy

Folding and holding
the smell of September now
in the wind and whisper
of my girl when I miss her

I wish to stop time when I'm with her
illustrating her every curve with my eyes
in the movement that rocks this artist's hand
drawing fixation creation

I will turn you
into eternity
tracing you in tribute
on walls everywhere

You are my power
you are the stroke
of passion
and pulse

My motion makes you
in the mist of dots
that creates you
and lines of waterfall hair

The smell of you is still left in my ears
And so obscure is the range at which I hear you
because our sound travels
through the tickles from far gone

This catharsis manual
draws with it
the phone buzz earphone
lightly tapping the unsaid

PLEASANT VIEW

Pleasant view
Black in the sun
Sleeping on the road
Side of your face
In the light, flicker

House of music
Back roads to the new
Clutch and fuel hard
Let it ride in classic
Living in pattern, rest

Philadelphia faces in brisk
Pennies for our thoughts
The Neptune chilly cheeks
And the lives of lovers
In just a few weeks, streets

Strolling the streets
Two dollars for a guitarist
A good man to rock on, man
Perplexed and disgusted
Lines of remedy, laugh

Flat notes and fake gloats
Drag us down from a beauty, unmatched
To sail the streets
The highway defeats
To south in winds of ice and Keansburg

January Coronas and Loretta slang,

For sure, are these beats of R&B soul, rising

The dances we teach each other

In the ghost town of sand and snow

Carry my eyes in the groove you sway

WOE

For sure, for here
We rise in the Queen,
The brand of our gleam

So much hair since August
In the daily rush of a clear
Collision to your kisses

No time remains for the tangible;
The racket of the dreams that creep and crawl
From the livid and the lively goal of the soul

This work is a crowd of agnostic, atheist adolescents
Wandering to wander
And wooing from wonder

BLANK SLATE

With spokes the wheel turns
In definite and finite
The candle it burns
For losing to learn

Amiss, the blinding fire
Of the late afternoon star
Through my window
Calls to me

Energy-anxiety seethes as I breathe
For it is not the shadow of darkness
That makes my heart bleed with
Prickling numbness on this slate of the day

It is the food of your number
Behind and beyond the four o' clock clouds
Which is the distance between
Life-to-live and live-that-is

KISSED BY CHRIST

Today, a beauty confusing
Kissed by Christ
And coughing the gray diamond stone
From my lungs

I hear the voice of a butterfly and
Feel the wounds of the Healer
Broken by the stories from my dreams
Of the Owl Child

Spiritual reflections on this day of peace
Bring me the confidence to conquer the king of the hills
Here, hiding the horror of the human hunt and
The hatred of this dark basement beneath the chapel of choices

On the first day of the rest of this life, afternoon breaks;
The time of trials and the months that star and start with terror
Will soon, but not soon enough,
Melt away the madness of the mission

SKY DRAGON

At 38,000 feet in a Spirit can,
A bus in the sky,
Are my mucus-filled ears awry

The hum-drum drone of the digital sky dragon
Seems as numb as I
And from my Xanax dream I comply

Orlando on the way to welcoming the can
Of annoying, anxious mumbles
Of so many Florida travelers,

Where the sum of 127 small bottle top air vents
Blast their stale, semi-cool personalities throughout the cabin
And the stench of *I've-got-nothing-better-to-do-than-complain-and-cackle-useless-sounds-from-my-face* words that penetrate the atmosphere

So, I turn to my purple-shirt lady
And she is sleeping against the window
With her profile distinguished so smoothly

By the vibrant blue and bright white
Fluffy vastness upon which we glide
In this vessel

ELECTRIC SKIN

Radiant music and sounds are hissing
beyond the walls in this darkness breathing
and in the stillness of the calm
is the rise in my eyes to this clicking.

My woman's sleep and deep breathing
next to me in the warmth of this bed
stick to the lights of electronics in my head
as I click the buttons of this device so dead.

Ritualistic prayers of Middle Eastern cultures
fade in and out
through the shadows and apartment walls
like preying vultures.

Screams in Spanish from the street below
and mufflers of cars whizzing by so low
are like far off lagoons of liquid lies
that whisper in my ears with distant despise.

So I lay in this cave with street light shadows
where my skin is empty like the guilt of the gallows
and I wonder with each day that passes
if I will rise once again in this world with my electric skin glasses.

GOLD

Winter faces in plastic, peddled haze
In the lamp light luminance of this magnetic, mental daze
Stretch down into the binding belly of my brawn
And wait their stay until each is released under the cover of dawn

Yet in this mid night nectar,
as I lay in the warm embraces of my angel,
The snow and sleet covered windows they do tangle
While these eyes see no less than the shimmering gold
Of the delicate glow of her sugar sweet hair so bold

ZERO

Fahrenheit has no bearing
on this winter tearing
through the fruits and fluid
of our silent, sour druid
of drains and ice so nice
if the night could ever be good
here in the hood

The chance of our survival
is as drab as the dread we feel
for the emptiness of dead in the head
of the wild boars we are
to rip through and ravage our dreams
as we snore the bore away this day
pray and have faith in the force of all
above and beyond this wall of sleep
and lay to waste our ignorance.

ELIXIR ENGINE

Wizards wait and warriors wallow
Through the swordsman's clank
And the maiden's vixens they follow

The roaring of iron on the famous stags
Meet the hell of battle
And the tourniquet wild

But low down behold this engine of rage
Feeding the rags upon ready
This potion and the heavy

Of armor and steel is this soldered slave
Marching onward and fearless
Until the holy grave

THE RUINS OF NEW JERSEY

This rain pours here and now upon the brow
The lack of light and lack of youth washing away
And feeding the ground and gravel under plow
As rivers of soot form around the soil this day

The ruins of New Jersey in gray clouds form
Urban and suburban in rural fields worn
Driving in the paths of fog and frame
These pictures are the images of Earth's swollen veins

Hunger and chill descends through active ends
Instill the still when the cross-fade of life bleakly mends
Ancillary active in the arcade of hissing wind transcends
This place of plush anatomy rush

This state of plenty and shards of room
So wicked is this wicker engine balloon

MELANCHOLY MOMENTS

Reality subjective is amiss tonight
For it breaks me down savagely if this is the spirit
Muffled in barriers of malaise, tectonic
Giving in to the surrendering soul's collapse upon it

Back lit boxes of the books my head
Pave paths and carnage of withering wires in this bed
While the smell of coconut cream and its slippery scent
Wafts in the air like candle flames capture
The jumping eyes in the dark of the room

Purpose is what plights us
In this post-impossible me
And reaches the roundabout
In words I hope to see

Easy now it is to tell
That sticky is the smoke that clings to my skin
Resting is my body while covering the covers
But the mind meanders and melts
In much more than these melancholy moments

CHASING THE SUN

Chasing the sun with stereo punch
Top Down and a Metallica lunch

Photographs in the glare
Stick shift on the highway, and her hair

Day of the Resurrection, heading south
Toward the sun, we finally open the sky's mouth

We meet the Parkway with stale flow
Traffic-bound, and our faces aglow

FLORIDA DREAMS

Florida dreams are the sunshine state of mind
These thoughts are the creatures that dwell in this place of mine

Unfortunate bloodsuckers they are
Leaving their marks on the skin they scar
Such skin that bubbles with blisters from the fire of the star

Piercing the clouds and mist through our atmosphere far
Their blades reach me and cover me cooked
While the devil's vampire bugs I have overlooked

Such a mess, I confess
Jumbled and compounded by this
Are my battles with battles within my head that rattles

The past is the past, and I ponder this ramble
That swirls in the sunshine of my state of mind
What better times are these when swirling with such ease?

SALVE, MADRE

Salve, Madre
Life of my Father
Godmother of Grace
Where no one would bother

Mother of mine
The world, your twine
Cuore di un santo
And the language of Love

Chiesa di Dio
And God is gracious with you
Più venerato dai santi
The legends of mothers that be

Patron of builders, with grace, siete pieni di
And the stones the heart's artillery
Pray for us all with your power
In the candle – della vita – so tall

THE DIVE

Night falls without her and she is gone
Behind the glass grayscale, craving the stale
When she falls into these dull obscure fields
In black flowers and white wind, this raw infinite

Snowing salt-and-pepper television she is
Saving her hair-feathers and cannot be reached in this mist
Forgotten gloss inside this box with none lasting beyond Never
So I will dive into the narrator and become black-and-white

She heaves her pulsating prowess and wild flavor
Giggling into the tract of darkness and taste
Shadows watching and smashing glass in celebration
We dive into the walls where wet is dry and skin is fire

YOLKS AND NUMBERS

There's something buried under here
I dream about it every night, but there's nothing I can do about it:
The planet provides the sugar in the bacteria to the root
and the bacteria is very sensitive to too much oxygen

I want to plant some seeds in my garden soil
because I had approximately two mishaps last night
You see, in a food chain the key is energy-flow
and Nitrogen and Phosphorus are very limiting

There can be two to three levels of carnivores
Very interesting, but nevertheless I need the food
and very flammable protozoa
to break down the organic matter

The more hatchlings there are, the more food there is
Not to mention that pinecones release the seedlings after the fire
When you eat... you eat a little of yourself,
Then you lose yourself... when you defecate

We are the Eukaryotes here, you see,
With a membrane to protect us
Because the Flu is a blob virus that changes every year
when true parasites must live inside your cells

Viruses have the protein and the DNA to eat
and prions are the puzzle to the science prison
Therefore, they are the Mad Cow Disease...
They are the protein in numbers

Egg yolks and Epsom salts do make a great omelet…

The clear area will turn green and harvest worms –

– nothing healthy there…

Except an artificial ecosystem

THE TREE CLIMBER

I was standing on the horizon
Where the trees were hairs on an arm
I took an axe and chopped one down, but it started to bleed
Because I was too close to the skin

There was an earthquake and he shook the pain from his elbow
I had to hold on to the cut so that I wouldn't fall
But accidents will happen
And his veins exploded, releasing toxins from his blood

His blood was filled with scuba divers
And tiny maggots that looked like fish
I ran across the scars left by childhood
But when I got to the wrist it was open,

And a man with a top hat crawled out of the wound and said,
"Don't go in there, son, it's dark."

I then realized that this was no place for a tree climber,
So I grabbed my axe and shined it with my shirt
Until I could see my face in it
I looked really deep into the reflection
And then I reversed myself into it
Now I was inside the reflection of my axe
Where everything was purple and green

I saw myself on the other side, but I didn't look back at me

THE NIGHT

Dance with me on the blue beach
Where the sky glows eclectic
And earth shakes in quakes in response to rhythm

Ramble on with me about nothing in particular
Except why it is that it pours when it rains,
Like a universe falling

The aisles of sand fade me here
In the cotton clouds of the deep
Where every shell reminds me of you

You are always a part of me
In a vast ocean of cascading flowers
Drifting into a silent supernova

I go to the stars with my eyes
Yet the sky is so arrested with the lights of a city
And the clouds, a blanket of burnt orange

There is a reflection into my heart of the song
Of this earth and sea of perfect world, not so perfect
Without you

In raindrops falling down upon miles of exhausted fields
Like spontaneous memories
And these reflections into the glass I stare upon

I stand in the circle of many circles
That form the likes of countless others
And reveal the unknown world that is my world

I am this body of earth and world
In a place where the ground has no flesh
And, here, I am weightless among the star-lit open

I become one with the night
And the Night watches the world stroll
Through the motion of movement in the midst of mass

While the green stands firm amid the black
And the moon's body hovers
In the clouds that caress their shadows

To illuminate the night's journey and gems
In waves of shadow in the night's life turning
But the Night is powerless without branches

This Night's calm, like a never-ending dream,
Transcends the hours that have no echo
Calling me home to the pinhole in the sky

REBIRTH

I have found my way across the sun
I have traveled beyond oceans undone
In my canoe of fire I have ridden the tides
On the surface of the sun where heaven abides

I stare at it deep and directly through
What I find in the center – is you
Come with me now on my bright canoe
And step right into my shining new
One night with you – indelible and true

I'll weave the flames around your hair
That makes it gold, and your skin so fair
Your lips are waving, and call me home
Forever now, we are blissful – unknown

LINCOLN MAN

The Town Car pulls up to the house
Huge and white like an elephant mouse

At the high cement curb
It purrs like a cat

Our little black dog runs to the door
Her claws on the kitchen tiles like tic-tacs falling on the floor

In the dog's excitement for you, her eyes are raised
Petting her with your hands that are powerful and praised

You lean down to the boy because you tower
A testament to why people before you cower

The aftershave from your face
Lingers for hours all over the place

The vanilla and smoke clings to your jacket
When you are in our house among the joyous racket

Pressed to your chest, the boy hugs back
And walks away from the window to hang your coat on the rack

THE WATCHER

He stumbles to his place of rest
And falls deeply into epiphany and Earth's epitaph
Capturing him cloudless

Hanging heavy, his eyes roll like planets
Into the back of his head
Clasping for Cambridge

He sees so many stories that have no end
And only begin with Our oblivion
As he heads for the Pages

Wishing is he
That his books of words will go on forever
Such that they will mean something to someone, sometime

After the questions become, again and again,
Monotonous and milky with Mother Life
The Arms of Theory do open truths:

Alone has many faces, uncountable faces
And wonderful Internet protocol,
Looking lovely with the computer on

Skin tones searching the limitless non-linear
Scratching the background opaque
And the human, ultimate form

We drift into cyberspace dreams
Behind the liquid crystals and RGB
Talking madly to the glowing, galaxy screensavers

Our beach at the end-saver
Of the world darkened by excess tech
Soars and excels on the chill of solitude, limitless

On the balcony of the final minute
Nine floors above the sand pixels
Comes death in the icy, salt-earth liquid

Cresting on the castle canvas of desktop pictures
Inward and behind the glass We are
Overlooking Our distance, and drowning happily

Too much television, cyber-boxes, and after-images
Fill and fixate our world of war and pornography
On plastic and pieces of truth that stagger with Us tightly

Skin and hair and mud-soaked earth
Press to the shore bed, crusted with rot
Where memory rises like the ocean tide

Saltwater and skin, in one pupil dilation,
Are swimming in shreds to the mainland tugboat
Against the island face toward the hope of freedom

With such pale blue and whitewashed red
On the rapid rocks settling the setting
Dark and exposed is Life, and what life was

The ridiculing rain mist
Washes Us all away again
Like a slice of stationary circumstance

Leaving behind the words of gray like an appalling statue
Tied to a sinking steamboat
Where smoke in bubbles dissipates

The Watcher watches his stonewall pillars
That exceeds the sky clouds ever so silently
Succumb to the hurricane Death

Arched and beveled for nothing but nonsense navigation,
Gradations of absolute non-color
Arrive in winds of wicker knives and invisible density

The heavy-head horizon sinks loudly,
Leaving Our city capsule castle behind
And carving urban, sub-human pandemonium
into the devil's 3AM darkness

Staring with Emptiness
The Darkness is cold and wet and has no face
Dripping tar and fragments of beauty

Turned black from charred flesh
Quivering and calling out of its ragged head
Are screaming echoes of many a muses
That we swear we have heard before.

Half asleep and dream-writing, he watches
The absolute monument of catastrophe
When awful sounds of the infatuation of nothingness and despair
Creep in crescendos of a constant orchestra

So he reaches again for his sky's eye
And, by chance, he happens upon himself
And the untouched rhythm of All
While dark follicles of contorted curvature rain down

The Watcher and the Distant Destroyer battle
As we sleep silently away our hot breath
And the moist whispers of our cold,
Empty dreams.

APRIL

The outlook is fairly fair today
The ultraviolet index is fairly high
And humidity rises fairly above forty percent

Fair winds from the south
Move fairly at seven miles per hour
While tornado storms erupt in Louisiana

Our barometer here in New Jersey reads in
At fairly thirty point one nine inches
At one twenty-three in the afternoon

Sitting in a Moroccan oil-scented salon by the window
What's fair is fair
And all seems fairly well at that

Sweet-smelling aromas of women's hair products
Are juxtaposed to the hissing and howling of hair dryers
And murmuring gossip underneath it all

These happenings enlighten and accentuate
The dull goings on
Of this particular Saturday

This light purple, button-down shirt, daily-worn,
Black cargo pants of faded glory, and sneakers tied tightly
And double-knotted, never match anything else

Occasionally sipping stale coffee, black-and-sweet,

From its silly Styrofoam cup

This oversized purple shirt monster hangs ever so curled

Over his tightly-belted pants,

Hiding physical insecurities

But creating others

He basks in a vision of a goddess seated under the afternoon light

With flowing, heated strands of golden hair, fair

Not far from the direction of the machine finessing the air

AMERICAN DAZE

The haze of these American days is hard to escape
The rain clouds of democratic demons
Living wildly their power to devour

Ignoring tainted horror lips,
The devil's kiss and the apple
We pacify

Until paper disintegrates
Into the electronic pulp
Of modern machines

And the sweet Nanny
In a corrupt corner of the concrete mountain
Zaps the skull of the world until we collectively end

THE CALLING

Crucifix hanging high, and the broken lights above this sky
Stars in our eyes awry
Why then can we hear not
The call of our Father, distraught
So be it, we run and strafe
Because well known to us is the faith
Our Mother's friend, who is never late
On that journey to Earth, so we wait
When, and if, we walk together, so clever
Somehow the senses of you fall forever

And year thirty-three becomes the wind

Explosions on poles and towers light up the sky
Nature and earth growl and lightning does cry
Like foul faces, not human, and torched
We admire the detriment of this great, terrible scorch
Because well-made is this land afar
For whispering terrors of tyranny scar
Take this advantage, all who may listen
And in your eyes a shimmer of hope may glisten
Clear the conscience for a kiss from her fair
Allowance for love, not flesh, don't despair

GRIM

The ranting and raving of a madman
May be chilling when sanity is subjective,
A stark reminder of the multiverse revelation

Plot and story are the things of importance
For we are the story and the stories
Because exposition is the question

This was told to me once by a man made grim
And, for him, there was nothing more important
Than him

For him, what was grim
Was anything other
Than him

And those who knew him
Called him
Grim

HERO

Harrowing, hellish head
Underneath this happening hair
Hereto the hyper-happy is hindered
Halting heroism with this age

No more is the forward-thinking
Stagnant and stale is the self that stopped
Used and clamoring in this clinging crest
Of Christ and cigarettes, so cold and clasping

A flat-line fallacy faltering on a feather is this life
Now floating far in the fields of farce and finite
It is a struggle to find inspiration by inspiring the minds
Of these poor, lost, young, and misguided souls

So hell-bent toward hell themselves
Hell-set on acceptance and anger
Their fight is weakening and their plight is withering
So I hang on and live by the words of my Muse,

"The greatest accomplishment in life is wisdom and inner peace."

PATRIOT

Tyrannical rats of discourse and disdain
Rattle the graves of soldiers they stain
And dance in dizzy dollops of acid rain

Carbon monoxide vents in rusted pipes
Are their mouths of rhetoric and gripes
To bring public nausea and spin their crane

But we see our soldiers' epitaphs read,

All who step here beware.
My wrath far surpasses true evil compare.
Take up your arms! Behind you we stand!
We died with our freedom intact with this land!
Take it all! Take it fast! Take our lives that we give!
But nothing can kill our spirit, because through it we live!

ABOUT THE AUTHOR

Award-winning film producer and editor Joe DeVito III, founder and owner of Mariano Films, is writer, producer, and director of short and feature-length motion pictures in a wide variety of genres and styles. DeVito's motion picture company, Mariano Films, is the creative engine behind dynamic, engaging stories with positive messages using the industry's current camera technology. Accompanied by artists and filmmakers of all disciplines, DeVito maintains a creative, collaborative, and family-oriented atmosphere of filmmaking success that carries through his work and through his company. "In a world saturated with digital media," said DeVito, "it is very easy to lose sight of meaningful storytelling and the importance of the craft of filmmaking. Nowadays anyone can pick up a camera and make a film, but few can tell a great story that drives the spirit. And that is always my goal."

Since the early 1980s DeVito has appeared as an actor in stage plays and independent films. He has worked as a producer and editor on films ranging from short subject documentaries to major motion pictures. In 2003 DeVito worked for Cataland Films in New York City with acclaimed producer Richard Perello for the film *Brooklyn Rules*, starring Alec Baldwin, Freddie Prince Jr., Scott Caan, and Mena Suvari. Two years later he became the co-owner of Forward Features, a cutting-edge digital video production company that produced documentaries, music videos, and an array of media services for worldwide corporate clients. Under this company he achieved recognition at the Tribeca Film Festival for the film entitled *Humanoid*, about a defective robot that was purchased under false pretenses. He continued producing films that spawned an underground fan-base across the U.S. for their quirky and unusual humor.

When Mariano Films was created in 2007 DeVito's company moved into larger collaborations with major studios, musicians, and producers at HBO, Fox Searchlight, Warner Brothers, and Nickelodeon. Mariano Films was recognized in 2008 for the short comedy film *Handicapped*, a movie advocating the rights of disabled persons, as well as the documentary *Open 24 Hours*, an inside look at the New Jersey diner culture. DeVito also collaborated with New Jersey Pictures as a producer and editor for the documentary *We Love You*, headed by three-time Academy Award® Nominee Steve Kalafer, and worked side-by-side with director Jonathan Kalafer. "The story of this film, and being a part of its creation, changed my life," said DeVito. The film was awarded "Best Documentary" at the Los Angeles International Short Film Festival and "Best Short Documentary" at the New Jersey Film Festival in 2009. *We Love You* documents the 2008 Rainbow Gathering in Wyoming. Every summer since 1972 thousands of people co-create a temporary city deep in the wilderness of our national forests, where people are there to practice anarchy and hippy spirituality. The main event is an elaborate prayer for peace on July 4th. But the Rainbows' peaceful ways are challenged when federal agents charged with monitoring them shoot pepper spray projectiles into the children's' area of the gathering.

DeVito's next project with Jonathan Kalafer was working as an associate producer for the inspiring, feel-good documentary *Once in a Lullaby: The PS22 Chorus Story*, about a group of fifth graders that went from performing in their school auditorium on Staten Island, New York to closing the show at the 83rd Annual Academy Awards. It all started when their dynamic and caring teacher, Gregg Breinberg, began posting videos of their performances on YouTube. The videos went viral, captivating viewers from your house to the White House (where they performed for the President) with the students' pure love of music. Celebrities and Indie Rockers alike started flocking to the elementary school to visit and perform. Then, at their annual Christmas concert they got a surprise visit from Oscar Co-Host Anne Hathaway who invited them to perform at the 83rd Annual Academy Awards. With unprecedented access the film crew followed them from the hallways and streets of Staten Island to the Red Carpet and backstage at the Kodak Theater for their big Oscar performance. This documentary story shows us that children have a lot to teach about music, and that a talented teacher can teach his students the most important lesson of all; within one's self is the power to accomplish anything. The film premiered as an "Official Selection" at the Tribeca Film Festival and won "Best Documentary" at the New Jersey Film Festival in 2012.

In addition to leading Mariano Films, Mr. DeVito is a certified educator of the visual arts and teaches high school in New Jersey. He heads a dynamic digital arts curriculum that includes digital filmmaking, digital photography, digital design, and digital media. He also teaches art fundamentals, as well as a course in portfolio development for aspiring future artists. His educational web site is at www.**DeVitoArt.com**, and his motion picture company web site is found at www.**MarianoFilms.com**.